Your Body and Health

MUSCLES

Jen Green

STARGAZER BOOKS

© Aladdin Books Ltd 2006

Produced by: Aladdin Books Ltd

*First published in the
United States in 2006 by:*
Stargazer Books
c/o The Creative Company
123 South Broad Street
P.O. Box 227
Mankato, Minnesota 56002

Printed in Malaysia

Editor: Katie Harker

Designer: Simon Morse

Illustrators: Aziz A. Khan, Simon Morse,
Rob Shone, Ian Thompson

Cartoons: Jo Moore

Certain illustrations have appeared in
earlier books created by Aladdin Books.

Medical editor: Dr. Hilary Pinnock

*Dr. Pinnock is a GP working in England. She
has written and consulted on a wide variety
of medical publications for all ages.*

*Library of Congress Cataloging-in-
Publication Data*

Green, Jen.
    Muscles / by Jen Green.
      p. cm. -- (Your body and health)
    Includes index.
    ISBN 1-59604-056-4
      1. Muscles--Juvenile literature. I. Title.

QP321.G775 2005
612.7'4--dc22
                        2005042529

Contents

Introduction

Did you know that without your muscles, you would be a stiff heap of bones and jelly lying on the floor? Muscles allow your body to move and to do all sorts of things, such as kicking a ball or lifting a heavy load. The special system that makes these things possible —the muscles—also keeps your heart beating and helps you breathe and talk. This book tells you all you need to know about your muscles and how to keep them in good shape for a healthy body.

Medical topics

Use the red boxes to find out about different medical conditions and the effects that they can have on the human body.

You and your muscles

Use the green boxes to find out how you can help improve your general health and keep your muscles in tiptop condition.

The yellow section

Find out how the inside of your body works by following the illustrations on yellow backgrounds.

Health facts and health tips

Look for the yellow boxes to find out more about the different parts of your body and how they work. These boxes also give you tips on how to keep yourself really healthy.

What are muscles?

Muscles provide the power you need to move your body. They pull on your bones so that you can carry out many different actions. Muscles also pump life-giving blood around your body and help you to breathe and to digest food.

All animals move with the help of muscles. Kangaroos have strong muscles in their back legs that enable them to make giant leaps.

The word "muscle" comes from the Latin word *musculus,* meaning "little mouse." The ancient Romans thought that rippling muscles looked like little mice running under the skin!

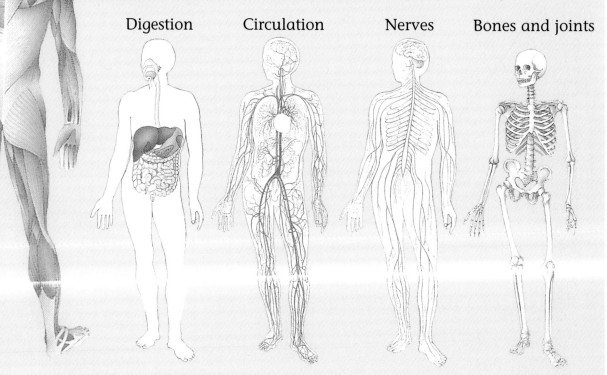

Muscles

Systems of the body

Our bodies are often described in terms of separate systems, each with a different job to do. However, each body system is dependent on the others to work at its full potential. One important system—the muscles—takes oxygen and nutrients from your circulatory system and works alongside your bones and joints to give your body movement.

Digestion   Circulation   Nerves   Bones and joints

Where are your muscles?

Muscles make up about two-fifths of your body weight. Muscles are found all over your body, from your face and limbs to inner organs such as the heart, stomach, and lungs. You can control the movement of most of your muscles, but others work automatically inside your body.

Voluntary muscles are muscles that you can move whenever you want to. They include the muscles attached to your bones (skeletal muscles) that give your body shape and enable you to move, balance, and hold heavy objects.

Involuntary muscles work automatically inside your body. You cannot control involuntary muscles. They include your heart muscle and the smooth muscles that move food through your digestive system and help control the flow of blood in your blood vessels.

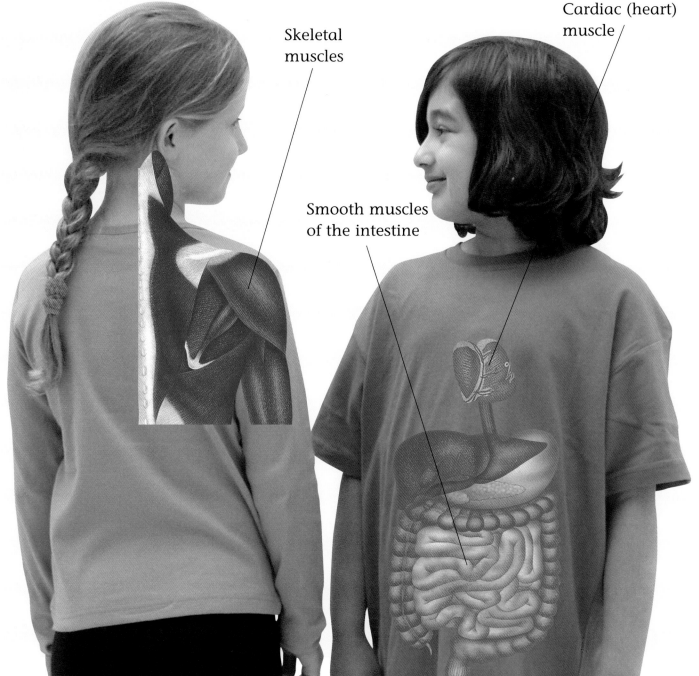

Skeletal muscles

Cardiac (heart) muscle

Smooth muscles of the intestine

What do your muscles do?

All the muscles in your body have different jobs to do. Skeletal muscles are attached to your bones. They are used to move your body and to give your body strength. Cardiac muscles keep your heart beating so that your blood flows around your body. Smooth muscles line the walls of your internal organs to keep your body parts moving and in good working order.

The smallest muscle is 0.04 inches (1mm) long—the stapedius muscle inside your ear. It tightens when you hear a loud noise to prevent damage to your inner ear.

Movement

When you want to move, your brain sends a signal to your skeletal muscles. Your muscles contract and because they are attached to your bones, they help you to carry out all kinds of movements.

Breathing

Two types of muscles help you to breathe: the intercostal muscles between your ribs, and your diaphragm, a sheet of muscle attached to the bottom of your rib cage. When these muscles tighten and relax, they pull on your ribs and change the volume of your lungs. Air is sucked in and forced out in the process.

Ribs move down and inward

Intercostal muscles

Diaphragm moves up

Facial expressions

You have hundreds of muscles in your face which help you to scowl and smile. These muscles are tiny so that you can produce the delicate movements needed for a whole range of facial expressions. Smiling uses about 20 facial muscles, while frowning uses over 40.

Strength

Your muscles support your body and give you strength so that you can carry heavy objects and move your body in a range of different positions. Activities like mountain climbing (left) require both strength and endurance, to keep your body supported over a long period of time.

Pumping blood

Your heart muscle sends blood pumping around your body. This muscle is especially strong because your heart has to beat all the time. The walls of your major blood vessels also contain smooth muscle. Your body adjusts these muscles to control the flow of your blood.

Keeping things moving

Smooth muscles control the movement of your internal organs. They are found in the walls of your blood vessels and the lining of your airways and tubular organs like your stomach and intestines. These are the muscles that help to churn your food and move your urine from your kidneys into your bladder.

Muscles of the skeleton

One of the largest muscles in the body is the one you sit on, the gluteus maximus, in your buttocks.

Skeletal muscles are found all over your body, from your face to your fingertips. You have about 640 skeletal muscles in total. Some skeletal muscles work together with your bones so that you can carry out complicated actions, such as leaping and running. Others are attached to body tissues to allow you to perform more delicate movements, like blinking.

Main skeletal muscles

Your skeletal muscles are mostly arranged symmetrically —with one on the right side and its twin on the left side of your body. Skeletal muscles have several layers which make them both strong and flexible. Some of the most important muscles in your body are shown here.

Deltoid

Triceps

Gluteus maximus

Hamstring

Gastrocnemius

Tendon

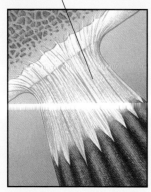

Tendons

Tendons are tough bands that keep your muscles attached to your bones. They are made of strong, stringy fiber, rather like a very tough rope. Fibers in the tendon merge with muscle fibers at one end and are embedded in bony tissue at the other end.

Tendons

Large muscles

The large muscles in your legs, back, shoulders, and arms are used in movements involving strength, such as lifting a weight or swinging a racket. They also help with energetic movements, such as jogging and running upstairs, or actions that require a force, like throwing.

Small muscles

Smaller muscles in the face, wrists, hands, and fingers are used to carry out delicate, skillful actions, such as talking, holding a pencil, or chewing food. Many small muscle skills need good hand-eye coordination, like balancing cards or painting.

Pectoralis major

Biceps

Abdominals

Blood vessel

Adductors

Sartorius

Quadriceps

Belly

Tibialis anterior

Muscle structure

Most muscles have a bulging central part (or belly). They get narrower at the ends, where tendons attach them to bones. Muscles are supplied with blood vessels that bring nourishment and oxygen and remove waste material. They are also linked to nerves that relay signals from the brain.

Skeletal muscle shapes

Skeletal muscles are different shapes and sizes. Most skeletal muscles are long and thin, designed to give your body frame a wide range of movement as the muscles contract and relax. Other skeletal muscles cover a broader area but do not pull as hard because the muscles contract and relax in different directions. Circular muscles are designed to close openings in the body.

The Achilles' tendon in the heel is named after the legendary Greek warrior Achilles, who died after being wounded in his heel.

Moving bones

Most of your larger muscles connect to more than one bone. When this happens across a joint, fibrous tissues, called ligaments, fasten your bones together while the action of your muscles pulls your bones apart or together. Ligaments are like bands or sheets as strong as rope.

Muscle shapes

Spindle-shaped muscles include your biceps and your calf muscles. Sheets of flat muscle in your chest and back tighten and relax to help you breathe. Strong triangular muscles in your shoulder allow you to move your arms. A small, strap-shaped muscle in your throat helps with talking and swallowing. Circular muscles in your lips open and close your mouth.

Shoulder muscle (deltoid)

Back muscle (latissimus dorsi)

Lip muscle (orbicularis oris)

Upper arm muscle (biceps)

Muscle linking throat and breastbone (sterno-mastoid)

Weak muscles

Muscles waste away (shrink) if they aren't used regularly. This can happen if you break a limb and have to rest it while it heals. Muscular dystrophy is an inherited illness that causes muscles to weaken. The disease can cause difficulty walking or breathing. Special tests measure muscle strength (right), and braces or exercises can help to keep muscles as strong as possible.

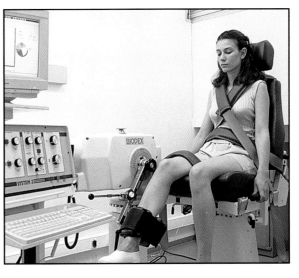

Achilles' tendon

The Achilles' tendon connects your calf muscle to your heel bone. The Achilles is one of the longest and strongest tendons in your body but it can be subjected to a number of strains, particularly when playing sports. Common injuries include a torn or inflamed tendon, causing pain and swelling.

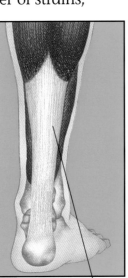

Calf muscle (gastrocnemius)

Achilles' tendon

Muscle names

Every muscle in the body has a scientific name, based on Latin, that is understood by doctors everywhere. The names of muscles often reflect the work they do. Muscles called flexors flex or bend joints. Muscles called extensors extend or straighten joints. Rotator muscles make joints twist or rotate.

Rotators flex and rotate the elbow.

Flexors pull and flex the wrist forward.

Extensors bend back the wrist.

11

Skeletal muscle pairs

Skeletal muscles shorten to pull on bones, but they cannot push against them. Another force is needed before a muscle can relax and get longer. This is why many muscles are arranged in pairs, one on each side of a bone. The muscle pair works as a team: one muscle pulls the bone one way and then relaxes as its partner pulls the bone back again.

Muscle pairs pull against one another like antagonists (opposite sides) in a tug-of-war contest. They are called antagonistic pairs.

Muscle balance

Every day you use a number of different muscles to move around. It is not uncommon to use one part of a muscle pair more than the other. This muscle imbalance sometimes occurs naturally—for example, by doing lots of actions in front of your body where you can see what you are doing, such as sitting hunched over a computer for a long period of time. Sleeping in an uncomfortable position can also put extra stress on individual muscles, making them feel stiff or sore. Stretching and relaxing both parts of the muscle pair again will help to regain a healthy balance.

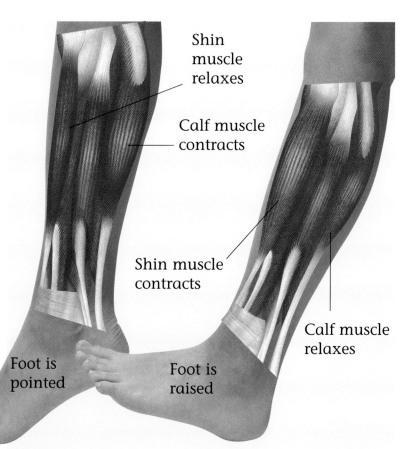

Shin muscle relaxes

Calf muscle contracts

Shin muscle contracts

Calf muscle relaxes

Foot is pointed

Foot is raised

Leg muscle pairs

The shin and calf muscles in your lower leg form a pair that allows you to raise your heel and walk on tiptoe, or plant your heel and raise your toes. To raise your heel, your calf muscle contracts, while your shin muscle relaxes. To raise your toes, your shin muscle tightens, while your calf muscle relaxes.

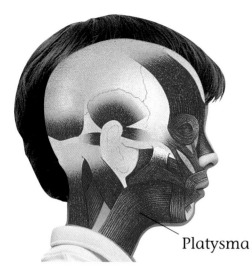
Platysma

Missing muscles

Many people are born without certain muscles. For example, some people do not have a platysma —a facial muscle that runs from below the chin to the chest and shoulder. If your platysma is missing, you will have a less pronounced chin. These naturally occurring variations are generally harmless, but some missing muscles can lead to a restriction in body movement.

Flex arm

The biceps and triceps muscles in your upper arm work as a team, just like your shin and calf muscles. As you raise your forearm, the biceps muscle at the front tightens and the triceps muscle relaxes. As you lower your arm again, the triceps muscle at the rear contracts while the biceps relaxes. As well as lifting and lowering, other muscle pairs move your limbs apart and together, or forward and backward.

Biceps flexes and triceps relaxes, bending the arm.

Triceps flexes and biceps relaxes, extending the arm.

Inside muscles

Some jellyfish have muscular tentacles that contract very strongly. A fully stretched tentacle can measure 66 feet (20 m) long, but contract to just 5 inches (13 cm).

All muscles work by contracting (getting shorter) and relaxing. As muscles contract, they get fatter. You can see the biceps muscle in your upper arm bulging as you bend your arm. This is because muscles are made up of lots of tiny threads. These threads overlap when a muscle contracts, and spread out again as the muscle relaxes and gets longer.

Physical therapy

Physical therapy is a treatment to help heal damaged muscles or to strengthen weak muscles. A physical therapist may massage damaged muscles, use ultrasound to help muscles heal quickly, or prescribe exercises to improve muscle strength.

Muscle filament (magnified)

Muscle filament

Muscle filament

Muscle fibril

Muscle makeup

Skeletal muscles are made of long, thin strands called fibers, bound together in bundles. Each fiber contains smaller strands called fibrils, which are made up of even finer threads called filaments. Muscles are protected by a tough covering called a sheath.

Muscle fibers

Muscle fibers are long, thin cells about the thickness of hairs. A large, bulging muscle can contain hundreds of these thin fibers. A small, slender muscle may contain no more than twenty fibers. Muscle fibers are bound together in bundles called fascicles. Each bundle is supplied with blood vessels that bring nourishment and remove waste products.

Sheath

Muscle fiber

Blood vessel

Muscle bundle (fascicle)

Pulling power

There are two kinds of muscle filaments: thick threads made of a protein called myosin, and thinner threads made of a protein called actin. These filaments overlap as muscles contract and lengthen as they relax.

Stripes

The tiny filaments in your muscles, made of the proteins actin and myosin, look striped when seen under a microscope. For this reason, skeletal muscles are sometimes called striped or striated muscles.

Muscles of the limbs and torso

The longest muscle is the sartorius muscle in your thigh—up to 12 inches (30 cm) long. Sartorius means "tailor's muscle" because it moves the body into a cross-legged position once used by tailors.

The central part of your body is called your torso. It contains many powerful muscles, including the wide, strong muscles in your hips and shoulders that move your arms and legs. Your limbs have long, slender muscles that make them light and flexible. Small muscles in your arms, wrists, and fingers allow you to grip objects tightly or carry out delicate tasks.

Tennis elbow

Tennis elbow is the name given to an inflammation of the area around your elbow joint. It is traditionally caused by playing racket sports, but can affect non-tennis players too!

Torso muscles

Strong muscles in your neck balance your head and enable you to turn it to the left or right. Wide muscles in your shoulders and upper chest allow you to raise and swing your arms. Flat muscle sheets around your stomach protect the soft parts of your digestive system. The lower torso muscles let you bend your body forward or lean over to one side.

Neck muscles

Shoulder muscles

Chest muscles

Stomach muscles

Lower torso muscles

Arms and legs

Your upper body muscles are much smaller than your leg muscles, which are constantly working when you stand up or walk around. The largest muscles in your arms are the shoulder muscles. These lift the weight of your arms. If you walk or cycle a lot, you will develop larger calf muscles as your muscles work harder and become stronger.

Shoulder muscle

Calf muscle

Reflexes

Reflexes are quick, automatic movements that protect you from danger. Your brain constantly sends and receives signals from parts of your body via the spinal cord. In a reflex reaction, your spinal cord immediately reacts to signals from your senses and instructs your muscles to move. In the meantime, other signals continue to your brain so that you know what's happening. If your eyes spot a ball whizzing straight at you, your arm may move up automatically to protect your head.

Balance

Your brain, senses, and muscles work as a team to keep your body balanced. The eyes, inner ears, and other sensors in the body send messages about your position to the brain. The brain responds by instructing your muscles to move to keep you balanced, whether you are running, walking a tightrope, or riding a bike.

Muscles of the face

Your jaw muscles have a number of different uses. Without them you wouldn't be able to bite, chew, or talk!

The muscles in your face, head, and throat enable you to breathe, eat, talk, and also sing and whistle. The powerful muscles in your jaw enable you to bite and chew. You move many smaller muscles in your face as you grin, scowl, or put on other expressions. Tiny muscles in your eyes, ears, nose, and tongue help you to see, hear, smell, and taste.

Smiling and scowling

Some of your face muscles are attached to your skin or to other muscles, not to your skull bones. When you smile, zygomaticus muscles running from your cheeks to the edges of your lips tighten. This pulls the corners of your mouth up. When you frown, corrugator muscles in your forehead contract to wrinkle your brow.

Frown

Smile

Corrugator

Zygomatic major

Zygomatic minor

Making a face

Facial expressions allow you to show your feelings. You can make lots of silly faces, too! Small muscles in the face move your eyebrows, mouth, and other features a fraction of an inch up, down, or sideways as you glare, blow your cheeks out, show wide-eyed surprise, or put on a silly grin.

Talking muscles

The muscles of your throat, jaws, lips, and tongue are used in speaking. Air passing up your windpipe is vibrated by two muscular bands in your throat called the vocal cords. These vibrations produce sounds, which are then shaped into words by your lips, teeth, and tongue.

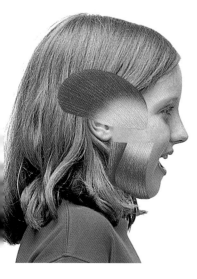

Eye muscles

Six small, straplike muscles attach your eyes to their sockets. These teams of muscles make tiny movements to adjust the position of your eyes, so you can look up, down, or to the side. Smooth muscles also work inside your eyes to keep them focused when you look at things close up or far away.

Eating muscles

You have two pipes in your throat—the windpipe which leads to your lungs for breathing, and the esophagus, or food pipe, which leads to your stomach. Muscles pull a flap called the epiglottis over the windpipe as you swallow, to make sure your food goes down the right way.

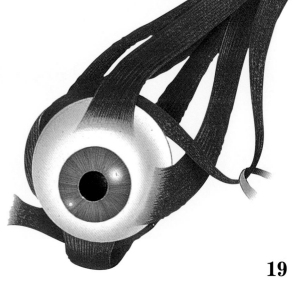

Involuntary muscles

Your brain can take control of some involuntary muscles, such as your breathing muscles, when you play the tuba.

Involuntary muscles are muscles that work automatically, without your having to think about them. They include muscles that carry out vital body functions, such as circulation and digestion; cardiac muscles that keep your heart pumping; and smooth muscles that line your intestines and help move food through the digestive tract.

Pulse rate

Every time your heart beats it pushes blood through your arteries, which you can feel as a pulse. Your pulse rate is a measure of your heart's activity. When you rest your pulse rate is low, but when you are active your pulse rate will increase.

Heart muscle

The cardiac muscles in your heart never stop working. They contract and relax constantly to pump blood around your body. As the heart muscles relax, blood flows into your heart from your veins. As the heart muscles contract, blood is forced out of the heart into arteries that lead to the rest of the body.

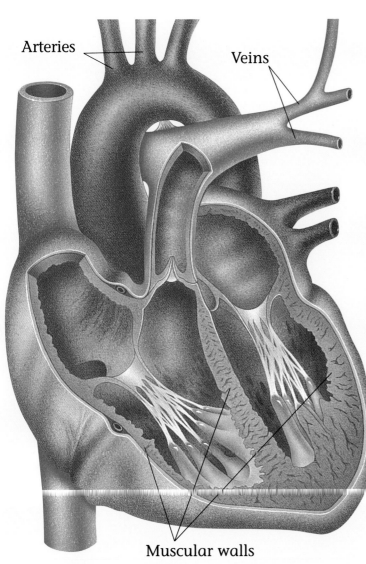

Arteries

Veins

Muscular walls

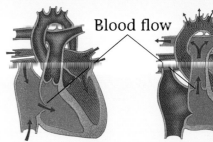

Blood flow

Relaxed muscle   Contracted muscle

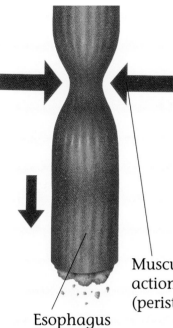

Digestive muscles
The esophagus (food pipe), the stomach, and the intestines are all lined with smooth muscle. Food in your stomach is squeezed to a pulp by the muscular walls. The walls of your intestines also contract in regular waves to push food through your digestive system. They move in a wavelike action called peristalsis.

Muscular action (peristalsis)

Esophagus (food pipe)

Small intestine

Stomach

Food

Muscular walls

Keeping active
Regular exercise makes your heart and lungs work harder, which strengthens your heart and breathing muscles. If you excercise regularly you will also develop stronger skeletal muscles and improve your flexibility.

Rib muscles

The intercostal muscles between your ribs help your diaphragm to force air in and out of your lungs during breathing. As you start to breathe in, the intercostals contract to pull your ribs up and outward. This expands the space inside your lungs to draw air in. As the intercostals relax, they move the ribs down and inward. This forces stale air out.

Moving your muscles

Curare is a plant sap from South America that paralyzes muscles. Amerindian hunters used to dip their arrows in this natural poison.

Skeletal muscles are also called voluntary muscles because you can order them to move when you want to. They are under the control of your conscious brain. When you decide to make a movement, your brain sends a signal down a pathway called a nerve to the appropriate muscles. When the muscles receive the signal, they contract. Another signal makes them relax again.

Muscle messages

Skeletal muscles are controlled by an area in the brain called the motor cortex. These movement centers in the upper brain relay messages to nerves via your spinal cord. Throughout the body, nerves link with muscles at tiny junctions called motor end plates. When the signals pass the junctions, the muscles contract.

Motor cortex

Spinal cord

Multiple sclerosis

Multiple sclerosis (MS) is a disease that damages nerves throughout the body. The illness interrupts messages between the brain and the body's nerves (right), making it difficult to control some muscles. Symptoms vary, but include muscle weakness, numbness, and loss of coordination. Although there is currently no cure for MS, medicines and other treatments can reduce the severity of symptoms.

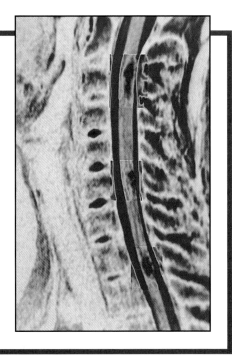

Memory

Your muscles are able to carry out all sorts of complicated movements under guidance from your brain. With training, your brain can also remember a complex set of actions, like the skills needed to play a musical instrument, juggle, ride a bicycle, or play soccer.

Motor nerve sends signals to muscle

Learning new tricks

Your brain can teach your muscles to do two different actions at once! Try rubbing your stomach and patting your head at the same time. Now swap hands! The new movement is difficult at first, but the brain and muscles soon adjust.

Taking care of muscles

A good
night's sleep
rests tired
muscles that
have been
on the go
all day.

Oxygen and glucose (also called blood sugar) provide the fuel that powers your muscles. Glucose comes from the food that you have digested. Oxygen comes from the air you breathe into your lungs. Both oxygen and glucose are carried in your bloodstream to muscles all over your body. In working muscles and other cells, glucose is broken down to release energy.

Cramp

A cramp is a painful muscle contraction that sometimes strikes if you work your muscles too hard. It may also happen if you hold your body in an awkward position. The affected muscle goes into spasm—it contracts but will not relax again. You can usually ease cramp by rubbing and stretching the affected part.

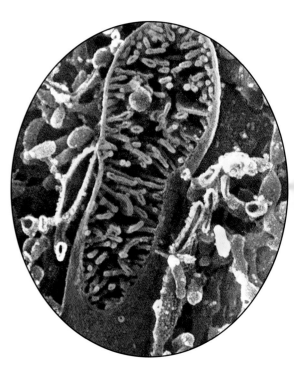

Energy source
Energy is released inside tiny parts of muscle cells called mitochondria (shown above). The process uses up oxygen and produces the waste gas carbon dioxide. Carbon dioxide enters your blood and is carried back to your lungs so you can breathe it out.

24

Anaerobic exercise

Exercise that involves short bursts of exertion followed by periods of rest (for example, sprinting or weight lifting) are called "anaerobic." These exercises use up oxygen faster than the lungs can supply it, and develop stronger, more flexible muscles.

Muscle fatigue

When athletes train hard, lactic acid may build up in their muscles. This is especially common following anaerobic exercise. Your muscles may feel tired or ache after exercise because they are in need of more oxygen. This is why athletes breathe heavily and have a fast heart rate shortly after exercising. Rest helps to cure the problem.

Food for muscles

Carbohydrates, like pasta, are a good fuel for your muscles. Protein, like meat, helps to repair damaged muscles, and low-fat foods, like fruit and vegetables, develop leaner, stronger muscles.

Aerobic exercise

Exercises that make your heart and lungs work hard to supply your muscles with oxygen are called "aerobic." These exercises strengthen your heart and lungs and improve your overall fitness. Dancing, jogging, and cycling are all forms of aerobic exercise.

Muscles in sports

Exercise makes you hot. Take care not to cool down too quickly. Marathon runners put on foil blankets so they don't get chilled after a race.

The more you use your muscles, the stronger and more fit you get. However, you need to do both anaerobic and aerobic exercise to maintain general fitness. Exercising your muscles at high intensity for short periods of time will help to increase the strength and the size of your muscles. Exercising at low intensity for longer periods will keep your heart and breathing muscles fit and healthy.

Strength, not size
Good technique is just as important as brute strength in some sports. If you train hard to improve your skill and coordination, you can often do just as well as, or even better than, someone twice your size.

Warm-ups

Warm-up exercises help to loosen your muscles and flex your ligaments and joints before you play sports or start serious training. These stretches and bends are important to avoid any injury. Doing the same exercises after you exercise helps your body to warm down and recover after sports.

Torso bend (1) strengthens torso and hip muscles. Stand with your feet apart. Keeping your legs straight, slide one arm down your leg as far as you can. Now try the other side.

Leg stretch (2) loosens hip and leg muscles. Step forward, then lean forward on the front leg to stretch the muscles in your back leg. Hold for a while, then try the other leg.

1

2

Speed

Increasing your muscle strength and endurance will help you to make muscle movements more quickly. Sprinters or hurdlers (left) do weight and endurance training to keep their muscles in top condition. If they can train their muscles to use oxygen efficiently, and if they can keep their muscles moving quickly, they will be more likely to win their race!

Endurance

Endurance is your ability to keep exercising over a long period of time. Long-distance runners (right) train their muscles so that they can run for a long time without getting tired. General fitness helps their muscles use oxygen efficiently.

Agility and balance

Your muscles work together to support your body and help you to balance, such as when you sit, stand, and walk. Gymnasts strengthen their muscles so that they can balance when performing different routines.

Strength

Anaerobic exercise, like weight training (below), increases the numbers of actin and myosin filaments in your muscle fibers. This increases the size and strength of your muscles, making you stronger.

Sports injuries

When training for any sport, you should always start gently and build up gradually, to avoid injuries. If you try to do too much too quickly, you may end up at the doctor's, not the finish line! Warming up properly, wearing the right equipment, and following instructions will also help you to get the most out of exercise.

Staying healthy

When lifting a heavy weight, always keep your knees bent and your spine straight. Lift the weight gently to avoid hurting your back.

Without your muscles, you wouldn't be able to move at all—one reason to take good care of them! A varied low-fat diet with plenty of fruit and vegetables helps to keep your muscles in good condition. Regular exercise is also vital to keep muscles in trim. Dancing, cycling, swimming, walking the dog, ball sports, or a workout at the gym—the choice is yours!

Drink water

Your body needs water, from your food and drink, to keep it hydrated. When you exercise, you lose water as you sweat, so you need to drink even more. Without water your body cells cannot work properly to keep your body healthy. Take a bottle of water with you when you exercise.

Wear the right gear

For many sports, you need to wear the right sort of footwear. Sometimes this is to support your ankles when you perform energetic activities, so you don't tear or sprain any muscles. Some sports require extra gear, such as helmets and protective padding. Avoid injury by buying, borrowing, or renting the right equipment.

Aches and pains

Pay attention to any aches and pains that develop when you are exercising. If you feel a sharp pain, stop at once. Don't try to stretch a strained muscle—you could do more damage. A hot, relaxing bath will help cure minor muscle strains. If a muscle pain continues, see your doctor for advice.

Cooling down

After sports, "cooling down" exercises help to relax your muscles and keep your joints supple. Jog slowly in place and do a few bends and stretches. Shake your arms and legs, and gently flex your neck and spine.

Keeping active

As you get older, your body changes. Muscles tend to weaken, joints may become less flexible, and some of your muscle tissue is replaced by fat. Regular exercise NOW will help you to stay fit for longer.

Food for life

Eating a balanced diet and drinking plenty of water will give your muscles the nutrients that they need to keep you active. Carbohydrates give your muscles energy, and proteins build and maintain your muscles as you grow. Try to eat a low-fat diet to keep your muscles lean and strong, but remember that your muscles also need small amounts of fat for energy.

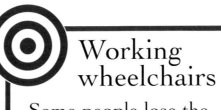

Working wheelchairs

Some people lose the use of certain muscles through illness or an accident. If the leg muscles or spine are affected, they may get around by wheelchair. Many wheelchair users lead fully active lives. A number of sports have been adapted for wheelchairs and are now included in the Paralympics.

Amazing facts

Astronauts who spend a lot of time in space are likely to get weak because they don't have to work against gravity. Space vehicles are fitted with exercise machines to help astronauts keep their muscles strong.

Daily exercise can increase the size of your muscles by up to two-thirds.

Skeletal muscles make up almost half of the body weight of a very fit person. In a person who is unfit, they may only make up a third.

Most of an animal's flesh is skeletal muscle. When you eat meat, you are actually eating muscle.

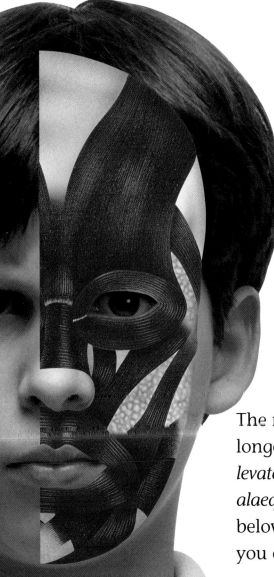

The muscle with the longest name is the *levator labii superioris alaeque nasi*. This muscle, below your nose, helps you curl your upper lip.

Glossary

aerobic exercise Any form of exercise that makes the heart and lungs work to supply muscles with oxygen. "Aerobic" means "with oxygen."

anaerobic exercise Very strenuous exercise that makes the muscles use energy without oxygen. "Anaerobic" means "without oxygen."

antagonistic muscles
A pair of muscles that pull against each other, such as the calf and shin muscles in the lower leg.

artery A blood vessel that carries blood away from the heart.

cardiac muscle The strong muscle that keeps the heart pumping.

cramp A painful involuntary muscle contraction that may be caused by overuse, heat, or cold.

fascicle A bundle of muscle fibers.

involuntary muscles Muscles that are not controlled by the conscious brain.

joint A place where two bones are connected.

ligaments Fibrous tissues that fasten bones together across a joint.

multiple sclerosis An illness that attacks the nerves, often affecting the control of muscles.

muscle fibers The long, thin cells inside skeletal muscles that are built to contract, or shorten. Inside muscle fibers are even finer strands called filaments.

muscle filaments The tiny threads inside muscles that slide over each other to shorten the muscle.

muscular dystrophy A disease that causes muscles to weaken and waste away.

skeletal muscles Muscles that are mostly attached to the bones.

smooth muscles The muscles that line the walls of inner organs, such as the stomach, intestines, and lungs.

tendons The long, stringy cords that attach muscles to bones.

vein A blood vessel that carries blood to the heart.

voluntary muscles Muscles you can control and move when and where you want them to.

Index

Photo credits
Abbreviations: l-left, r-right, b-bottom, t-top, c-center, m-middle

All photos supplied by Select Pictures except for: 4tr, 23c, 27bm, 27br, 28bl, 30t—Corbis. 7tl, 25t, 25m, 25bm, 29tr —Digital Stock. 11tr—BSIP, Laurent/ Science Photo Library. 14mr— Antonia Reeve/Science Photo Library. 14bl— Science Photo Library. 17ml— Larry Williams/CORBIS 23tr— BSP Ducloux/ Science Photo Library. 24mr— Professors P. Motta & T. Naguro/Science Photo Library. 25mr—Will McIntyre/Science Photo Library. 25br, 30br—Stockbyte. 27tl, 27ml, 27mr —Corel. 28mr—Tom Stewart/CORBIS. 29mr—Ariel Skelley/CORBIS.